EPHESIANS

Our Immeasurable Blessings in Christ

JOHN MACARTHUR

THOMAS NELSON
Since 1798

MacArthur Bible Studies
EPHESIANS

© 2007, John F. MacArthur, Jr.

Published in Grand Rapids, Michigan, by HarperChristian Resources. HarperChristian Resources is a registered trademark of HarperCollins Christian Publishing, Inc.

Requests for information should be addressed to customercare@harpercollins.com.

ISBN: 978-0-7180-3510-5

Printed in the United States of America.

CONTENTS

INTRODUCTION TO EPHESIANS

The letter is addressed to the church in the city of Ephesus, capital of the Roman province of Asia (Asia Minor, modern Turkey). Because the name Ephesus is not mentioned in every early manuscript of this letter, some scholars believe the letter was an encyclical, intended to be circulated and read among all the churches in Asia Minor and was simply sent first to believers in Ephesus.

AUTHOR AND DATE

No evidence has arisen for questioning Paul's authorship. He is indicated as author in the opening salutation (1:1; 3:1). Written from prison in Rome (Acts 28:16–31) sometime between AD 60–62, the letter is, therefore, often labeled a prison epistle (along with Philippians, Colossians, and Philemon). Ephesians may have been composed almost at the same time as Colossians and initially sent with that epistle and Philemon by Tychicus (6:21–22; Col. 4:7–8).

BACKGROUND AND SETTING

The gospel probably was first brought to Ephesus by Priscilla and Aquila, an exceptionally gifted couple (see Acts 18:26), who had been left there by Paul on his second missionary journey (Acts 18:18–19). Located at the mouth of the Cayster River, on the east side of the Aegean Sea, Ephesus was perhaps best known for its magnificent temple of Artemis, or Diana, one of the seven wonders of the ancient world. It was also an important political, educational, and commercial center, ranking with Alexandria in Egypt and Antioch of Pisidia, in southern Asia Minor.

Later, Paul firmly established this fledgling church on his third missionary journey (Acts 19), and he pastored it for some three years. After Paul left, Timothy pastored the congregation for perhaps a year and a half, primarily to counter the false teaching of a few influential men (such as Hymenaeus and Alexander), who were probably elders in the congregation there (1 Tim. 1:3, 20). Because of those men, the church at Ephesus was plagued by "fables and endless genealogies" (1 Tim. 1:4) and by such ascetic and unscriptural ideas as the forbidding of marriage and abstaining from certain foods (1 Tim. 4:3). Although those false teachers did not rightly understand Scripture, they propounded their ungodly interpretations with confidence (1 Tim. 1:7), which produced in the church harmful "disputes rather than godly edification which is in faith" (1 Tim. 1:4).

About thirty years later, Christ gave the apostle John a letter for the church indicating that its people had left their first love for Him (Rev. 2:1–7).

HISTORICAL AND THEOLOGICAL THEMES

The first three chapters are theological, emphasizing New Testament doctrine, whereas the last three chapters are practical and focus on Christian behavior. Above all, this is a letter of encouragement and admonition, written to remind believers of their immeasurable blessings in Jesus Christ, not only to be thankful for those blessings, but also to live in a manner worthy of them. Despite, and partly even because of, Christians' great blessings in Jesus Christ, they are sure to be tempted by Satan to self-satisfaction and complacency. Thus, in the last chapter, Paul reminds believers of the full and sufficient spiritual armor supplied to them through God's Word and by His Spirit (6:10–17) and of their need for vigilant and persistent prayer (6:18).

A key theme of Ephesians is the mystery (meaning a heretofore unrevealed truth) of the church—"that the Gentiles should be fellow heirs, of the same body, and partakers of His promise in Christ through the gospel" (3:6), a truth completely hidden from the Old Testament saints (3:5, 9). All believers in Jesus Christ, the Messiah, are equal before the Lord as His children and as citizens of His eternal kingdom, a marvelous truth that only believers of this present age possess. Paul also speaks of the mystery of the church as the bride of Christ (5:32; Rev. 21:9). Paul emphasizes the major truth that the church is Christ's present spiritual, earthly body, also a distinct and formerly unrevealed truth about God's people. This metaphor depicts the church not as an organization, but as a living organism composed of mutually related and interdependent parts. Christ is Head of the body, and the Holy Spirit is its lifeblood. The body functions through the faithful use of its members' various spiritual gifts, sovereignly and uniquely given by the Holy Spirit to each believer.

Another prominent theme is the riches and fullness of blessing to believers. Paul writes of "the riches of His [God's] grace (1:7), "the unsearchable riches of Christ" (3:8), and "the riches of His glory" (3:16). Paul admonishes believers to "be filled with all the fullness of God" (3:19), to "come to the unity of the faith and of the knowledge of the Son of God, to a perfect man, to the measure of the stature of the fullness of Christ" (4:13), and "to be filled with the Spirit" (5:18). Believers' riches in Christ are based on God's grace (1:2, 6–7; 2:7), peace (1:2), will (1:5), pleasure and purpose (1:9), glory (1:12–14), calling and inheritance (1:18), power and strength (1:19; 6:10), love (2:4), workmanship (2:10), Holy Spirit (3:16), offering and sacrifice (5:2), and armor (6:11–13). The word "riches" is used five times in the letter; "grace" is used twelve times; "glory" eight times, "fullness" or "filled" six times; and the key phrase "in Christ" (or "in Him") twelve times.

THE RICHES OF HIS GRACE

Ephesians 1:1–14

DRAWING NEAR

The book of Ephesians opens with praise and wonder at God's love and grace for His people. Yet we often fail to appreciate that love and grace ourselves. The famed nineteenth-century preacher Charles Spurgeon told a story of a minister who called on a poor woman with a desire to help her out of her financial straits. Money in hand, he knocked on her door repeatedly, but she did not answer. Eventually he left. Later, he related the incident to her at church. "Oh dear," she said, "I heard you, sir, and I'm so sorry I did not answer. I thought you were the man calling for the rent."

How does this story illustrate our tendency to misunderstand (and miss out on) the riches we have in Christ?

_____

_____

_____

Think about your own relationship with God. Have you ever responded or felt as this woman did? What things stop you from opening up your heart to all God has for you?

_____

_____

_____

As you begin this study, ask God to help you receive what He wants to give you.

_____

_____

_____

THE CONTEXT

Paul spent three years pastoring the church at Ephesus and instructing them in the things of God. During that time he probably taught them all the great truths of this epistle. Because of Satanic opposition as well as the human tendency to forget what is true, however, Paul sensed the need for a letter of reminder and encouragement. He wanted to challenge his brothers and sisters in the faith to grow in grace and to stand firm in the midst of an evil age.

Rather than beginning with a long list of dos and don'ts, Paul began his correspondence with a refresher course in theology, answering questions such as: How is salvation accomplished? Why did God bestow His grace on us? What does the future hold for those who put their faith in Christ?

Paul recognized that such an emphasis on difficult doctrines was necessary because God-honoring *behavior* always springs from right *beliefs*. Christians who lack a proper theological foundation will not have a proper appreciation for what God has done, nor will they adequately understand the resources at their disposal in the life of faith.

In the following passage, Paul describes believers' infinite blessings in Christ. Specifically he gives a panoramic view of God's great salvation.

KEYS TO THE TEXT

Predestination: Taught throughout Scripture, election is God's perfect plan for the destiny of His creatures; it conforms both with His love and grace and with human beings' responsibility to believe in Jesus as Lord and Savior. The energy that has driven God's plan of redemption from eternity past flows from the power of His love. He chose us and predestined us "in love" (Eph. 1:4–5). It is solely "because of His great love with which He loved us" that He raised us from our hopeless state of spiritual death (Eph. 2:4). Because He loved us with an everlasting love, He drew us to Himself (Jer. 31:3). Christ died because of God's love for us (Rom. 5:8). In other words, election is the highest expression of God's love to sinful humanity. Some people hate this doctrine. They try to explain it away or claim it's not fair. But in reality the doctrine of election is all about the eternal, inviolable love of God. Fairness is not the issue; *grace* is the issue. Election is the highest expression of God's loving grace. He didn't have to choose anyone. And He is, after all, God. If He chooses to set His love in a particular way on whomever He chooses, He has every right to do so. But for Christians, the knowledge that we are saved because of God's choice is the supreme source of security.

UNLEASHING THE TEXT

Read 1:1–14, noting the key words, phrases, and definitions next to the passage.

Ephesians 1:1–14 (NKJV)

1 Paul, an apostle of Jesus Christ by the will of God,
To the saints who are in Ephesus, and faithful in
Christ Jesus:

2 Grace to you and peace from God our Father and
the Lord Jesus Christ.

3 Blessed be the God and Father of our Lord Jesus
Christ, who has blessed us with every spiritual
blessing in the heavenly places in Christ,

4 just as He chose us in Him before the foundation
of the world, that we should be holy and without
blame before Him in love,

5 having predestined us to adoption as sons by Jesus
Christ to Himself, according to the good pleasure of
His will,

6 to the praise of the glory of His grace, by which He
made us accepted in the Beloved.

7 In Him we have redemption through His blood, the
forgiveness of sins, according to the riches of His grace

8 which He made to abound toward us in all wisdom
and prudence,

9 having made known to us the mystery of His will,
according to His good pleasure which He purposed
in Himself,

10 that in the dispensation of the fullness of the times
He might gather together in one all things in Christ,
both which are in heaven and which are on earth—
in Him.

11 In Him also we have obtained an inheritance, being
predestined according to the purpose of Him who
works all things according to the counsel of His will,

12 that we who first trusted in Christ should be to the
praise of His glory.

13 In Him you also trusted, after you heard the word
of truth, the gospel of your salvation; in whom also,
having believed, you were sealed with the Holy
Spirit of promise,

14 who is the guarantee of our inheritance until the
redemption of the purchased possession, to the
praise of His glory.

blessed (v. 3)—from the same Greek word as "eulogy," which means to praise or commend. It refers to God's kindness to us as well as the appreciation or thanks we express back to Him.

He chose us (v. 4)—This refers to God's pretemporal, sovereign act of electing who will be saved, a common theme in Paul's writings (Rom. 8:29; 9:11; 1 Thess. 1:3, 4; 2 Thess. 2:13; 2 Tim. 2:10).

adoption as sons (v. 5)—the spiritual act whereby God brings a regenerated believer into His own family (see John 1:12)

redemption (v. 7)—The Greek word means to "buy back" or "ransom." Used in a salvation context, it refers to Christ's death on the cross that paid the price required to purchase the elect from the slave market of sin.

dispensation of the fullness of the times (v. 10)—The Greek word translated "dispensation" is the word from which we get our English word "economy." It means God's perfect arrangement or administration of events and history to accomplish His plan. The phrase here refers to the millennial kingdom at the end of world history.

sealed with the Holy Spirit (v. 13)—The spiritual act in which the Spirit of God, at the time of conversion, indwells a new believer and secures and preserves his or her salvation.

1) From this passage, identify the past, present, and future aspects of God's work in our lives (vv. 3–6, 6–11, 12–14). Why do you think Paul takes such a broad view?

_____

_____

_____

_____

2) Go through and underline the various references to the members of the Trinity—God the Father, the Son, and the Holy Spirit. What unique role does each play in the salvation process?

_____

_____

_____

_____

3) Several times in these verses we are granted insights into God's purpose(s) for salvation. Why did God predestine us to adoption as sons (v. 5)?

_____

_____

_____

_____

4) What do you think "to the praise of the glory of His grace" (v. 6) means? How is this idea also reflected in the last phrases in verses 12 and 14?

_____

_____

_____

_____

(Verse to consider: 1 Cor. 10:31)

5) The text states clearly that God receives glory, pleasure, and praise from our salvation. What does Paul say that *we* receive from the gracious hand of God?

_____

_____

_____

_____

GOING DEEPER

Read Romans 3:21–26 for more insight into what Paul has to say about our salvation from the penalty of sin.

21 *But now the righteousness of God apart from the law is revealed, being witnessed by the Law and the Prophets,*

22 *even the righteousness of God, through faith in Jesus Christ, to all and on all who believe. For there is no difference;*

23 *for all have sinned and fall short of the glory of God,*

24 *being justified freely by His grace through the redemption that is in Christ Jesus,*

25 *whom God set forth as a propitiation by His blood, through faith, to demonstrate His righteousness, because in His forbearance God had passed over the sins that were previously committed,*

26 *to demonstrate at the present time His righteousness, that He might be just and the justifier of the one who has faith in Jesus.*

EXPLORING THE MEANING

6) How does this passage in Romans compare and contrast with the teachings in 1:7?

_____

_____

_____

_____

_____

7) Read Romans 15:7. In this verse, Paul reminds the Christians at Rome that they have been *received* (that is, "accepted") by Christ. This theme is echoed in 1:6. What is so significant about this concept?

_____

_____

_____

_____

8) What aspect of our salvation mentioned in 2 Corinthians 5:21 makes us acceptable in God's sight?

_____

_____

_____

_____

Truth for Today

During the great depression of the 1930s, many banks would allow their customers to withdraw no more than ten percent of their accounts during a given period of time because the banks did not have enough reserves to cover all deposits. But God's heavenly bank has no such limitations or restrictions. No Christian, therefore, has reason to be spiritually deprived, undernourished, or impoverished. In fact, he has no reason not to be completely healthy and immeasurably rich in the things of God. The Lord's heavenly resources are more than adequate to cover all our past debts, all our present liabilities, and all our future needs—and still not reduce the heavenly assets. That is the marvel of God's gracious provision for His children.

Reflecting on the Text

9) What one truth has impacted your life the most from this passage, and why?

_____

_____

_____

_____

10) Have you been living as though the "good news" of salvation is not all that good? If so, what specific steps can you take this week to live out your great salvation?

_____

_____

_____

_____

11) Take the time to write your own list of "riches of grace" and blessings for which you are thankful, and praise God for His love and grace in your life.

_____

_____

_____

_____

Personal Response

Write out additional reflections, questions you may have, or a prayer.

_____

_____

_____

_____

_____

_____

_____

_____

_____

_____

_____

_____

ADDITIONAL NOTES

2

Prayers That Please the Father
Ephesians 1:15–23

Drawing Near

Consider the following typical prayers of many Christians:

- "Lord, bless us today."

- "Father, please help me find a parking spot close to the entrance."

- "God, forgive me where I've failed You, and help me to live for You today."

What (if anything) is right about these prayers? What (if anything) is wrong with them? Explain.

_____

_____

_____

What part does prayer play in your daily life?

_____

_____

_____

The Context

While discussing the marvelous acts of God and the great spiritual inheritance that believers in Christ possess, the apostle Paul spontaneously erupts into prayers of thanksgiving and praise. Remember, this was a church that was near and dear to his heart (see Acts 20:17–38). His affection for this particular flock and his passion to see them grasp the glorious riches of grace drove him to his knees.

With a backdrop of God's cosmic plan of salvation and in light of eternity, Paul's intercession takes on a weighty quality. He makes no trivial requests here. These recorded prayers serve as a wonderful model for how to pray for those we love and for whom we have been given responsibility to care for in the faith. Inspired as they are by the Holy Spirit, they also reveal the priorities that are on God's heart for His people. Let's look now at the kind of prayer that pleases the Father.

KEYS TO THE TEXT

Prayer: Fellowship and communion with God involving adoration, worship, praise, thanksgiving, supplication, petition, confession, repentance, meditation, dedication, and intercession. Based on the confidence that God hears His children, Christian prayer is addressed to God as Father through and in the name of Jesus Christ, His Son. Prayer is drawn partly from the urgency of human needs and partly from the promise and challenge of God's Word. Personal prayer is shaped by the awareness of God's presence. Corporate prayer is the living breath of the church. Through prayer the church resists the assaults of Satan (Matt. 26:41; Eph. 6:13–20), receives the gifts of grace (Acts 4:31), seeks deliverance, healing, and restoration for the saints (Eph. 6:18; James 5:15; 1 John 5:16), supports evangelization (Col. 4:3–4), and hastens the return of the Lord (Rev. 22:20). (*Nelson's New Christian Dictionary*)

UNLEASHING THE TEXT

Read 1:15–23, noting the key words and definitions next to the passage.

love for all the saints (v. 15)—the hallmark of God's people (1 John 4:8, 20–21)

do not cease (v. 16)—an echo of the same idea found in 1 Thessalonians 5:17

spirit of wisdom and revelation (v. 17)—a disposition of godly knowledge and insight that is possible only for a redeemed, sanctified mind

enlightened (v. 18)—illumined or given light; a reference to the Holy Spirit's ministry of continually illuminating spiritual truth for the child of God

exceeding greatness of His power (v. 19)—The same awesome power that raised Christ from the dead and exalted Him into heaven is made available to every believer in Christ.

principality and power and might and dominion (v. 21)—terms used frequently in Jewish writings to designate the various ranks of angelic powers

Ephesians 1:15–23 (NKJV)

15 *Therefore I also, after I heard of your faith in the Lord Jesus and your love for all the saints,*

16 *do not cease to give thanks for you, making mention of you in my prayers:*

17 *that the God of our Lord Jesus Christ, the Father of glory, may give to you the spirit of wisdom and revelation in the knowledge of Him,*

18 *the eyes of your understanding being enlightened; that you may know what is the hope of His calling, what are the riches of the glory of His inheritance in the saints,*

19 *and what is the exceeding greatness of His power toward us who believe, according to the working of His mighty power*

20 *which He worked in Christ when He raised Him from the dead and seated Him at His right hand in the heavenly places,*

21 *far above all principality and power and might and dominion, and every name that is named, not only in this age but also in that which is to come.*

²² *And He put all things under His feet, and gave Him*
   to be head over all things to the church,
²³ *which is His body, the fullness of Him who fills all in*
   all.

1) What characteristic(s) of the Ephesians prompted Paul to be thankful?
Why?

_____

_____

_____

_____

2) Underline in the passage the specific items (nouns) that Paul appealed
to God for on behalf of the Ephesian church. One request was that their
"spiritual eyes" might be opened, and thus come into a deeper knowledge of
God. Why was this foremost among the apostle's concerns for his flock?

_____

_____

_____

_____

_____

(Verses to consider: Isa. 6:1–8; John 17:3; Phil. 3:8–11)

3) How does Paul describe the power of God? Why is it significant that Paul
prays for the Ephesians to "know" this power rather than to "receive" this
power?

_____

_____

_____

_____

_____

GOING DEEPER

Read Colossians 1:9–12 and consider how Paul and his associates prayed for the Colossian believers under their care.

9 *For this reason we also, since the day we heard it, do not cease to pray for you, and to ask that you may be filled with the knowledge of His will in all wisdom and spiritual understanding;*

10 *that you may walk worthy of the Lord, fully pleasing Him, being fruitful in every good work and increasing in the knowledge of God;*

11 *strengthened with all might, according to His glorious power, for all patience and longsuffering with joy;*

12 *giving thanks to the Father who has qualified us to be partakers of the inheritance of the saints in the light.*

EXPLORING THE MEANING

4) In what ways does this passage specifically echo the Pauline teaching that right thinking leads to right living?

_____

_____

_____

_____

5) Colossians 3:2 says, "Set your mind on things above, not on things on the earth." How does this admonition relate to the manner in which Paul prayed?

_____

_____

_____

(Verses to consider: Matt. 6:33; 2 Cor. 4:18)

6) How should the truth that Christ is exalted above all (1:20–23) alter the way you live every day?

_____

_____

_____

TRUTH FOR TODAY

For Christians, prayer is like breathing. You don't have to think to breathe because the atmosphere exerts pressure on your lungs and forces you to breathe. That's why it is more difficult to hold your breath than it is to breathe. Similarly, when you're born into the family of God, you enter into a spiritual atmosphere wherein God's presence and grace exert pressure, or influence, on your life. Prayer is the normal response to that pressure. As believers we have all entered the divine atmosphere to breathe the air of prayer. Only then can we survive in the darkness of the world.

Unfortunately many believers hold their spiritual breaths for long periods, thinking brief moments with God are sufficient to allow them to survive. But such restricting of their spiritual intake is caused by sinful desires. The fact is, every believer must be continually in the presence of God, constantly breathing in His truths to be fully functional. God's deeper truths cannot be seen with our eyes, heard with our ears, or comprehended by our reason or intuition. They are revealed only to those who love Him.

REFLECTING ON THE TEXT

7) Someone has said, "The purpose of prayer is not to inform God of our needs, but to invite Him to rule our lives." Do you agree or disagree? Why?

_____

_____

_____

_____

8) In what ways do you need the eyes of your understanding to be enlightened? How can you begin fully appreciating the riches of God's grace in your life?

_____

_____

_____

_____

9) How would you assess your current prayer life? In what ways does it honor God? In what ways does it fail to honor God? What needs to change about the content and frequency of your intercession?

_____

_____

_____

_____

10) Write a prayer of thanks (or confession) to God in response to this lesson.

_____

_____

_____

_____

_____

PERSONAL RESPONSE

Write out additional reflections, questions you may have, or a prayer.

_____

_____

_____

_____

_____

_____

_____

_____

_____

_____

3

AMAZING GRACE!

Ephesians 2:1–10

DRAWING NEAR

One of the most debated religious questions is, "How does a person make it to heaven?" How would you answer that question?

_____

_____

_____

If you had to explain *grace* to a child, what would you say?

_____

_____

_____

THE CONTEXT

There are many different viewpoints on the question of eternal salvation. One common view says that *we* are individually responsible for our own destinies and how well we live determines where we will spend eternity. In other words, salvation is largely, if not entirely, dependent upon human effort. This view is popular because it appeals to human pride. It makes us feel in control. It gives us the sense that we can earn our own way. Besides, the notion of having to ask for help is galling to successful, independent people who see themselves as basically decent folks.

Another position says that salvation is a no-strings attached gift from God. We cannot possibly earn it, because we are sinful to the core. To paraphrase the words of C. S. Lewis, we are not basically nice people who need only to clean up our act a bit; rather, we are rebels who need to lay down our arms. Because of sin, we are spiritually dead. It's only when we respond to God's gracious overtures, admit our sinfulness and helplessness, and humbly receive Christ's offer of forgiveness and eternal life that we find life.

Obviously, this latter view is unpopular. It is an affront to self-made men and women who want to live without acknowledging or relying upon the Creator. Yet, as we will see in this lesson, *this* view is taught in Scripture.

KEYS TO THE TEXT

Grace: The only gospel of God is the gospel of grace, which is the gospel of divine redemption totally apart from any work or merit of man. We live in grace from the moment of salvation, and if grace ever stopped, we would lose our undeserved salvation and perish in sin. The grace of Christ is God's free and sovereign act of love and mercy in granting salvation through the death and resurrection of Jesus, apart from anything men are or can do. Not only does He freely give us this salvation, but He sustains it to glorification. It is absurd to accept a gracious salvation and then endeavor to maintain righteousness through human efforts, ceremonies, and ritual.

UNLEASHING THE TEXT

Read 2:1–10, noting the key words and definitions next to the passage.

Ephesians 2:1–10 (NKJV)

dead in trespasses and sins (v. 1)—total depravity and lostness resulting in an utter inability to know or please God

course of this world (v. 2)— a reference to the ungodly world structure, that system of entities and mind-sets that sets itself up against God and His rule

children of wrath (v. 3)—the rebellious unregenerates who stand condemned before God

rich in mercy (v. 4)—God lavishes compassion and pity on those He loves, despite their abject sinfulness.

made us alive (v. 5)—a reference to the supernatural act of regeneration, but also with the added nuance of sustaining and preserving life

workmanship (v. 10)—can have the connotation of a work of art

1 And you He made alive, who were dead in trespasses and sins,

2 in which you once walked according to the course of this world, according to the prince of the power of the air, the spirit who now works in the sons of disobedience,

3 among whom also we all once conducted ourselves in the lusts of our flesh, fulfilling the desires of the flesh and of the mind, and were by nature children of wrath, just as the others.

4 But God, who is rich in mercy, because of His great love with which He loved us,

5 even when we were dead in trespasses, made us alive together with Christ (by grace you have been saved),

6 and raised us up together, and made us sit together in the heavenly places in Christ Jesus,

7 that in the ages to come He might show the exceeding riches of His grace in His kindness toward us in Christ Jesus.

8 For by grace you have been saved through faith, and that not of yourselves; it is the gift of God,

9 not of works, lest anyone should boast.

10 For we are His workmanship, created in Christ Jesus for good works, which God prepared beforehand that we should walk in them.

1) How does Paul graphically describe those who are dead in sin? How does this compare to your experience before you became a Christian?

_____

_____

_____

_____

_____

(Verses to consider: Eph. 4:17–19; Rom. 8:10)

2) Underline the word *grace* used in this short passage. What other words does Paul use in the passage to describe God's actions toward the lost?

_____

_____

_____

_____

3) Ephesians 2:8–9 are the Bible's most concise statement of "salvation by grace through faith." This is the essence of the Christian gospel, and yet it has been the source of heated dispute. To what does the word *that* in verse 8 refer? What does it mean?

_____

_____

_____

_____

4) How are grace and faith related in our salvation?

_____

_____

_____

_____

GOING DEEPER

Paul talks more about what God has done for us in Romans 5:6–11.

6 *For when we were still without strength, in due time Christ died for the ungodly.*

7 *For scarcely for a righteous man will one die; yet perhaps for a good man someone would even dare to die.*

8 *But God demonstrates His own love toward us, in that while we were still sinners, Christ died for us.*

9 *Much more then, having now been justified by His blood, we shall be saved from wrath through Him.*

10 *For if when we were enemies we were reconciled to God through the death of His Son, much more, having been reconciled, we shall be saved by His life.*

11 *And not only that, but we also rejoice in God through our Lord Jesus Christ, through whom we have now received the reconciliation.*

EXPLORING THE MEANING

5) What themes in this passage from Romans echo the message of 2:1–10?

_____

_____

_____

_____

6) What is significant about the truth that God saved us at our worst, "while we were still sinners," or, in the words of chapter 2, when we were "dead in trespasses"?

_____

_____

_____

7) How does John 6:44 contribute to your understanding of this passage?

_____

_____

_____

TRUTH FOR TODAY

When we accept the finished work of Christ on our behalf, we act by the faith supplied by God's grace. When a person chokes or drowns and stops breathing, there is nothing he can do. If he ever breathes again, it will be because someone else starts him breathing. A person who is spiritually dead cannot even make a decision of faith unless God first breathes into him the breath of spiritual life. Faith is simply breathing the breath that God's grace supplies. Yet, the paradox is that we must exercise it and bear the responsibility if we do not.

REFLECTING ON THE TEXT

8) Charles Spurgeon wrote: "Faith occupies the position of a channel or conduit pipe. Grace is the fountain and the stream. Faith is the aqueduct along which the mercy flood flows down to refresh the thirsty sons of men. . . . I remind you again that faith is only the channel or the aqueduct, and not the fountainhead. We must not look to it so much that we exalt it above the divine source of all blessing which lies in the grace of God." Why is grace prior to and preeminent to faith?

_____

_____

_____

_____

9) What new insights have you gained through this study into the marvelous grace of God?

_____

_____

_____

_____

10) What can you do this week to "grow in the grace . . . of our Lord and Savior Jesus Christ" (2 Pet. 3:18)?

_____

_____

_____

_____

PERSONAL RESPONSE

Write out additional reflections, questions you may have, or a prayer.

_____

_____

_____

_____

_____

_____

_____

_____

_____

_____

_____

_____

_____

_____

_____

_____

_____

_____

_____

_____

_____

_____

_____

_____

_____

_____

_____

_____

_____

4

The Mystery of Unity in Christ
Ephesians 2:11–3:13

Drawing Near

It is part of sinful human nature to build protective barriers that shut out other people. What examples of disunity and division, segregation and schism, have you observed within the last month?

_____

_____

_____

_____

The Context

Ever since the rebellion in Eden shattered the relationship between humans and God, people have found it difficult to coexist peacefully. Every marriage, family, church (including the church at Ephesus), community, and nation struggles to maintain harmony and peace. Humanity's fallenness creates powerful feelings of alienation and suspicion, leading to prejudice, misunderstandings, disagreements, conflict, and even outright war.

It was no different in Paul's day. The early church consisted of Jewish people who believed in Jesus. Yet they still struggled to overcome prejudice against the Gentiles, the non-Jews, who were also becoming Christians. Paul showed them that Christ is the Prince of Peace and the key to unity in the church. He alone can bring us into right relationship with God. He alone can shatter the walls of prejudice and malice that separate human beings. Consider the amazing truth found in the following passage.

Keys to the Text

Gentiles: The Greek word used here is *ethnos*, from which we get our English term *ethnic*, and it signifies the non-Jewish world. In Paul's day, the Gentiles (the "uncircumcision") experienced two types of alienation. The first was social, resulting from the animosity that had existed between Jews and Gentiles for thousands of years. Jews considered Gentiles to be outcasts, objects of derision, and reproach. The second and more significant type of alienation was spiritual, because Gentiles as a people were cut off from God in five different ways: (1) They were "without Christ," the Messiah, having no Savior and Deliverer and without divine purpose or destiny. (2) They were "aliens from the commonwealth of Israel." God's chosen people, the Jews, were a nation whose supreme King and Lord was God Himself, and from whose unique blessing and protection they benefited. (3) Gentiles were "strangers from the covenants of promise," not able to partake of God's divine covenants in which He promised to give His people a land, a priesthood, a people, a nation, a kingdom, and a King—and to those who believe in Him, eternal life and heaven. (4) They had "no hope" because they had been given no divine promise. (5) They were "without God in the world."

UNLEASHING THE TEXT

Read 2:11–3:13, noting the key words and definitions next to the passage.

Ephesians 2:11–3:13 (NKJV)

11 *Therefore remember that you, once Gentiles in the flesh—who are called Uncircumcision by what is called the Circumcision made in the flesh by hands—*

12 *that at that time you were without Christ, being aliens from the commonwealth of Israel and strangers from the covenants of promise, having no hope and without God in the world.*

13 *But now in Christ Jesus you who once were far off have been brought near by the blood of Christ.*

14 *For He Himself is our peace, who has made both one, and has broken down the middle wall of separation,*

15 *having abolished in His flesh the enmity, that is, the law of commandments contained in ordinances, so as to create in Himself one new man from the two, thus making peace,*

16 *and that He might reconcile them both to God in one body through the cross, thereby putting to death the enmity.*

17 *And He came and preached peace to you who were afar off and to those who were near.*

18 *For through Him we both have access by one Spirit to the Father.*

the middle wall of separation (v. 14)—an allusion to a wall in the Jewish temple that separated the court of the Gentiles from the areas accessible only to the Jews

one new man (v. 15)—The Greek word translated "new" refers to something utterly unlike anything before it. The idea is that all who come to Christ comprise a new entity in which all labels, except the label "Christian," are obsolete. The believer is different in kind and quality. Spiritually, a new person in Christ is neither Jew nor Gentile but Christian only.

reconcile (v. 16)—to change or exchange; to turn from hostility to friendship

putting to death the enmity (v. 16)—The death of Christ killed the hostility between a holy God and sinful people.

19 *Now, therefore, you are no longer strangers and foreigners, but fellow citizens with the saints and members of the household of God,*

20 *having been built on the foundation of the apostles and prophets, Jesus Christ Himself being the chief cornerstone,*

21 *in whom the whole building, being fitted together, grows into a holy temple in the Lord,*

22 *in whom you also are being built together for a dwelling place of God in the Spirit.*

3:1 *For this reason I, Paul, the prisoner of Christ Jesus for you Gentiles—*

2 *if indeed you have heard of the dispensation of the grace of God which was given to me for you,*

3 *how that by revelation He made known to me the mystery (as I have briefly written already,*

4 *by which, when you read, you may understand my knowledge in the mystery of Christ),*

5 *which in other ages was not made known to the sons of men, as it has now been revealed by the Spirit to His holy apostles and prophets:*

6 *that the Gentiles should be fellow heirs, of the same body, and partakers of His promise in Christ through the gospel,*

7 *of which I became a minister according to the gift of the grace of God given to me by the effective working of His power.*

8 *To me, who am less than the least of all the saints, this grace was given, that I should preach among the Gentiles the unsearchable riches of Christ,*

9 *and to make all see what is the fellowship of the mystery, which from the beginning of the ages has been hidden in God who created all things through Jesus Christ;*

10 *to the intent that now the manifold wisdom of God might be made known by the church to the principalities and powers in the heavenly places,*

11 *according to the eternal purpose which He accomplished in Christ Jesus our Lord,*

members of the household of God (v. 19)—God's family

a dwelling place of God in the Spirit (v. 22)—In contrast to Old Testament times when God's presence was temporarily localized in the temple, now God takes up residence permanently in His church, the church.

partakers of His promise (v. 6)—The Gentiles share in the grace of God; this word was used in extra-biblical Greek to describe "joint possessors" of a house.

boldness and access (v. 12)—
Faith in an all-sufficient Savior
makes us acceptable to God and
is the basis of our access into the
presence of God.

tribulations (v. 13)—the fre-
quent pressures and troubles
that Paul encountered as he carried out his apostolic task (see
2 Cor. 11:22–29)

12 *in whom we have boldness and access with confidence through faith in Him.*

13 *Therefore I ask that you do not lose heart at my tribulations for you, which is your glory.*

1) How did Paul describe the spiritual plight of the Gentiles, and in what ways did the Jews have an advantage?

_____

_____

_____

_____

_____

(Verses to consider: Rom. 3:1–2; 9:4)

2) List all the "opposites" of being without Christ and being in Christ that Paul discusses (far off/but now near, etc). How do these illustrate the scope of what Christ had done for them?

_____

_____

_____

_____

_____

3) What was Paul's mission and call (3:6–9)?

_____

_____

_____

_____

4) In your own words, summarize the mystery revealed to Paul that he relates in this passage.

_____

_____

_____

_____

_____

GOING DEEPER

Consider how the following passage from 2 Corinthians 5:16–21 relates to the message of Ephesians 2:11–3:13.

16 *Therefore, from now on, we regard no one according to the flesh. Even though we have known Christ according to the flesh, yet now we know Him thus no longer.*

17 *Therefore, if anyone is in Christ, he is a new creation; old things have passed away; behold, all things have become new.*

18 *Now all things are of God, who has reconciled us to Himself through Jesus Christ, and has given us the ministry of reconciliation,*

19 *that is, that God was in Christ reconciling the world to Himself, not imputing their trespasses to them, and has committed to us the word of reconciliation.*

20 *Now then, we are ambassadors for Christ, as though God were pleading through us: we implore you on Christ's behalf, be reconciled to God.*

21 *For He made Him who knew no sin to be sin for us, that we might become the righteousness of God in Him.*

EXPLORING THE MEANING

5) What new insights does this passage add to the startling notion that in Christ *everything* changes?

_____

_____

_____

_____

6) If Christ is the Great Reconciler, and we are His "ambassadors," what does this mean? (What does an ambassador do?)

_____

_____

_____

_____

_____

7) What is the practical significance of the truth expressed in 2 Corinthians 5:17 for relational conflict in marriages, families, churches, and between races and nations?

_____

_____

_____

_____

_____

TRUTH FOR TODAY

During World War II a group of American soldiers was exchanging fire with some Germans who occupied a farm house. The family who lived in the house had run to the barn for protection. Suddenly their little three-year-old daughter became frightened and ran out into the field between the two groups of soldiers. When they saw the little girl, both sides immediately ceased firing until she was safe. A little child brought peace, brief as it was, as almost nothing else could have done. Jesus Christ came as a Babe to earth, and in His sacrifice on the cross He Himself became peace for those who trust in Him. His peace was not temporary but permanent.

God has always been deeply concerned about the unity of His people. By salvation, He has effected a real spiritual oneness. He has created a commonness based on sharing the same eternal life. This reality of conversion should impact the life of the church by being the impetus for practical unity.

REFLECTING ON THE TEXT

8) Why is the cross of Christ a true equalizer, and thus makes unity possible in the church?

_____

_____

_____

_____

_____

9) In *The Cross of Peace*, Sir Philip Gibbs has written: "Today there are all sorts of zig-zag and criss-crossing fences running through the races and peoples of the world. Modern progress has made the world a neighborhood and God has given us the task of making it a brotherhood." Is this just wishful thinking? How is this really possible?

_____

_____

_____

_____

_____

10) What act of reconciliation do you sense God leading you to pursue as a result of this study?

_____

_____

_____

_____

11) Make a list of wounded relationships for which you will pray for healing.

_____

_____

_____

_____

PERSONAL RESPONSE

Write out additional reflections, questions you may have, or a prayer.

_____

_____

_____

_____

_____

_____

_____

_____

_____

_____

_____

_____

_____

_____

_____

_____

_____

_____

_____

_____

_____

_____

_____

_____

5

The Power and Love of Christ

Ephesians 3:14–21

Drawing Near

It is important that we understand not only the truth of all that we possess in Christ, but also that we are divinely enabled to live out our great salvation. Do you feel sure of God's love for you? Why or why not?

_____

_____

_____

When have you felt God's power working in your life? How did you know? Explain.

_____

_____

_____

The Context

Many churchgoers are woefully ignorant of the vast spiritual wealth that is theirs in Christ. Others know a good deal about the Bible and the Christian faith, and yet fail to live by these truths. Either way, a meager spiritual existence is a tragedy, for as Paul reminded the Ephesians in the first part of his epistle, the children of God possess riches and resources beyond measure. We have the capacity to experience an abundant life (John 10:10).

In order for God to receive the glory He deserves and in order for us to find the fulfillment and purpose for which we were created, we need God to move in our hearts. We need illumination and motivation. This study looks at Paul's magnificent intercession for the Ephesians. In a passionate pastoral prayer, he gives a glimpse of the kind of rich existence that is possible when we are "filled with all the fullness of God."

Keys to the Text

Fullness of God: Being "filled with all the fullness of God" has to do with living out fully that which we already possess fully. It means to be so strong spiritually, so compelled by divine love, that one is totally dominated by the Lord with nothing left of self. Human comprehension of the fullness of God is impossible, because even the most spiritual and wise believer cannot completely grasp the full extent of God's attributes and characteristics—His power, majesty, wisdom, love, mercy, patience, kindness, and everything He is and does. But believers can experience the greatness of God in their lives as a result of total devotion to Him. When we trust in Christ, we are completely immersed into the Spirit and completely indwelt by Him. God has nothing more to put into us. He has put His very self into us, and that cannot be exceeded. What is lacking is our full obedience, our full trust, and our full submission—not God's full salvation, indwelling, or blessing.

Unleashing the Text

Read 3:14–21, noting the key words and definitions next to the passage.

Ephesians 3:14–21 (NKJV)

Father (v. 14)—Our awesome Creator is simultaneously a tender, loving, concerned, compassionate divine Parent who welcomes and invites His children to come to Him.

according to the riches of His glory (v. 16)—The limitless riches of God's power are available for the spiritual welfare of every believer.

strengthened (v. 16)—fortified, braced, invigorated

inner man (v. 16)—the real person as opposed to merely the outer physical appearance

dwell (v. 17)—to live in, to settle down in, to take up residence

exceedingly abundantly (v. 20)—beyond all measure; the highest comparison imaginable

14 *For this reason I bow my knees to the Father of our Lord Jesus Christ,*

15 *from whom the whole family in heaven and earth is named,*

16 *that He would grant you, according to the riches of His glory, to be strengthened with might through His Spirit in the inner man,*

17 *that Christ may dwell in your hearts through faith; that you, being rooted and grounded in love,*

18 *may be able to comprehend with all the saints what is the width and length and depth and height—*

19 *to know the love of Christ which passes knowledge; that you may be filled with all the fullness of God.*

20 *Now to Him who is able to do exceedingly abundantly above all that we ask or think, according to the power that works in us,*

21 *to Him be glory in the church by Christ Jesus to all generations, forever and ever. Amen.*

1) Why does Paul pray for the inner strength of the Spirit?

_____

_____

_____

_____

_____

2) What is the result of the fact that Christ dwells in our hearts through faith?

_____

_____

_____

_____

_____

3) What does it mean to "know the love of Christ which passes knowledge"?

_____

_____

_____

_____

_____

4) How are God's love and power related?

_____

_____

_____

_____

_____

_____

GOING DEEPER

Read Romans 8:31–39, a companion passage that sheds more light on the love of God.

31 *What then shall we say to these things? If God is for us, who can be against us?*

32 *He who did not spare His own Son, but delivered Him up for us all, how shall He not with Him also freely give us all things?*

33 *Who shall bring a charge against God's elect? It is God who justifies.*

34 *Who is he who condemns? It is Christ who died, and furthermore is also risen, who is even at the right hand of God, who also makes intercession for us.*

35 *Who shall separate us from the love of Christ? Shall tribulation, or distress, or persecution, or famine, or nakedness, or peril, or sword?*

36 *As it is written: "For Your sake we are killed all day long; We are accounted as sheep for the slaughter."*

37 *Yet in all these things we are more than conquerors through Him who loved us.*

38 *For I am persuaded that neither death nor life, nor angels nor principalities nor powers, nor things present nor things to come,*

39 *nor height nor depth, nor any other created thing, shall be able to separate us from the love of God which is in Christ Jesus our Lord.*

EXPLORING THE MEANING

5) How do God's actions confirm His love for us?

_____

_____

_____

_____

6) Nothing can separate us from God's love, Paul proclaims. What can you recall in Paul's experiences that would give him such confidence in and assurance of the love of Christ?

_____

_____

_____

7) In what ways does Psalm 96 depict more of the fullness of God?

_____

_____

_____

_____

_____

TRUTH FOR TODAY

God *is* love. His mercy is over all His works. He manifests His love to all. But the highest expression of His love is manifest to those who He lovingly draws to Himself by sheer grace. Therefore to those of us who believe, God's love is a uniquely precious reality, albeit an unfathomable one. There is no way we can scale the height of it. There is no way we can imagine the breadth of it or span the width of it. Nevertheless, by God's grace we can know the love of Christ, which passes knowledge (Eph. 3:18–19).

Why is all this so important? Ultimately the love of God is the basis for all our hopes. It is the source and fulfillment of our faith. It is the very basis for His grace to us. As Christians, then, we ought to see that everything we enjoy in life—from our tiniest pleasures to the eternal redemption we have found in Christ—is an expression of the great love wherewith God loved us (Eph. 2:4). The blessing of His love comes to us not because we deserve it, but simply and only because of His sovereign grace. For certainly we do not deserve His blessing, but the very opposite. Yet He pours out His love without measure, and we are invited to partake of its benefits freely. In light of the glories of divine love, how can we not be utterly lost in wonder, love, and praise?

REFLECTING ON THE TEXT

8) J. Wilbur Chapman often told of the testimony given by a man in one of his meetings. The man said: "I got off at the Pennsylvania depot as a tramp, and for a year I begged on the streets for a living. One day I touched a man on the shoulder and said, 'Hey, mister, can you give me a dime?' As soon as I saw his face I was shocked to see that it was my own father. I said, 'Father, Father, do you know me?' Throwing his arms around me and with tears in his eyes, he said, 'Oh my son, at last I've found you! I've found you. You

want a dime? Everything I have is yours.' Think of it. I was a tramp. I stood begging my own father for ten cents, when for eighteen years he had been looking for me to give me all that he had."

Like the father in the story, God has so much love and power to give. What keeps you from recognizing, and receiving, all that God has for you?

_____

_____

_____

9) What truth is most meaningful to you as you contemplate Paul's prayer for the believers at Ephesus?

_____

_____

_____

10) Using Paul's prayer as a model, write down ways you can intercede for people in your life this week.

_____

_____

_____

PERSONAL RESPONSE

Write out additional reflections, questions you may have, or a prayer.

_____

_____

_____

_____

_____

_____

_____

6

GOD'S PATTERN FOR THE CHURCH
Ephesians 4:1–16

DRAWING NEAR

The apostle Paul calls the church the "body of Christ." Why do you think that is a good metaphor?

_____

_____

_____

_____

In what ways does your church serve and work together as one body? In what ways does your church struggle with unity?

_____

_____

_____

_____

THE CONTEXT

After three chapters of solid instruction in the foundational truths of God, Paul takes a dramatic turn, shifting his emphasis from doctrine to duty, from principles to practice, from beliefs to behavior. He has set forth all the blessings, honors, and privileges of being a child of God. Now he reminds believers of their consequent obligations and requirements as members of God's family.

First, Paul explains to his beloved congregation in Ephesus that they must live up to their new identity and calling in Christ. Next, he describes the characteristics of true believers and how believers who are committed to the glory of God will live together in unity. This unity cannot occur unless each individual does his or her part. God has given each member of His church one or more gifts for the building up of the body. Corporately and individually we are to grow up and mature in faith, always on our guard against erroneous ideas spread by deceitful teachers.

To see how you can do your part to make your church all that God wants it to be, read and study the passage that follows.

Keys to the Text

The Body of Christ: The human body is by far the most amazing organic creation of God. While marvelously diverse and complex, it is yet unified, exhibiting unparalleled harmony and interrelatedness. Christ's body—the church—shares those same characteristics. Just as a human body has connected tissues, muscles, bones, ligaments, and organs, the body of Christ is comprised of members who are responsible to one another. No member exists detached from the rest of the body, any more than lungs can lie on the floor in the next room and keep a person breathing. The health of the body, its witness, and its testimony depend on all members faithfully ministering to one another.

Spiritual Gifts: The Greek word for *spiritual* literally means "pertaining to the Spirit," referring to that which has spiritual qualities or characteristics or is under some form of spiritual control. Spiritual gifts are divine enablements for ministry that the Holy Spirit gives in some measure to all believers. They are to be completely under His control and used for the building of the church to Christ's glory. The word *gifts* comes from the Greek word *charisma* and means essentially "gift of grace" or "free gift," and in sixteen of its seventeen New Testament uses is connected to God as the Giver.

Unleashing the Text

Read 4:1–16, noting the key words and definitions next to the passage.

Ephesians 4:1–16 (NKJV)

therefore (v. 1)—the transitional word that indicates Paul's shift from discussing doctrine to discussing duty

beseech (v. 1)—to call to one's side, with the intention of needing help; this word connotes strong feeling or desire and suggests pleading or begging

lowliness (v. 2)—a Greek word unique to the New Testament that describes the humble spirit that should mark all believers

gentleness (v. 2)—literally "meekness," strength under control, a mild spirit

longsuffering (v. 2)—literally "long-tempered," that is, patience

1 I, therefore, the prisoner of the Lord, beseech you to walk worthy of the calling with which you were called,

2 with all lowliness and gentleness, with longsuffering, bearing with one another in love,

3 endeavoring to keep the unity of the Spirit in the bond of peace.

4 There is one body and one Spirit, just as you were called in one hope of your calling;

5 one Lord, one faith, one baptism;

6 one God and Father of all, who is above all, and through all, and in you all.

7 But to each one of us grace was given according to the measure of Christ's gift.

8 Therefore He says: "When He ascended on high, He led captivity captive, And gave gifts to men."

9 (Now this, "He ascended"—what does it mean but that He also first descended into the lower parts of the earth?

10 He who descended is also the One who ascended far above all the heavens, that He might fill all things.)

11 And He Himself gave some to be apostles, some prophets, some evangelists, and some pastors and teachers,

12 for the equipping of the saints for the work of ministry, for the edifying of the body of Christ,

13 till we all come to the unity of the faith and of the knowledge of the Son of God, to a perfect man, to the measure of the stature of the fullness of Christ;

14 that we should no longer be children, tossed to and fro and carried about with every wind of doctrine, by the trickery of men, in the cunning craftiness of deceitful plotting,

15 but, speaking the truth in love, may grow up in all things into Him who is the head—Christ—

16 from whom the whole body, joined and knit together by what every joint supplies, according to the effective working by which every part does its share, causes growth of the body for the edifying of itself in love.

unity of the Spirit (v. 3)—the Spirit-bestowed oneness of all true believers

baptism (v. 5)—probably a reference to water baptism, post salvation

equipping of the saints (v. 12)—the act of restoring, making fit or complete; in this context, leading Christians from sin to obedience

no longer be children (v. 14)—God's expectation that spiritually immature believers should grow up in their understanding and behavior

every wind of doctrine (v. 14)—a reference to the beguiling spiritual error promulgated by deceitful teachers who lurked in the shadows of the Ephesian church (and still hinder God's work around the world today)

1) Paul begins this section of his letter with an urgent plea to "walk worthy of the calling" with which they had been called. What does he mean by this?

_____

_____

_____

_____

_____

_____

Circle the character qualities Paul mentions that will mark the life of a believer.

2) How does Paul describe the unity that believers ought to share?

_____

_____

_____

_____

_____

Underline every reference to unity that you see in this passage.

3) What obstacles can impede the spiritual growth and maturing of an individual Christian? Of a whole congregation?

_____

_____

_____

_____

_____

GOING DEEPER

For more on what it means to be the body of Christ, read Romans 12:4–18.

4   *For as we have many members in one body, but all the members do not have the same function,*

5   *so we, being many, are one body in Christ, and individually members of one another.*

6   *Having then gifts differing according to the grace that is given to us, let us use them: if prophecy, let us prophesy in proportion to our faith;*

7   *or ministry, let us use it in our ministering; he who teaches, in teaching;*

8   *he who exhorts, in exhortation; he who gives, with liberality; he who leads, with diligence; he who shows mercy, with cheerfulness.*

9   *Let love be without hypocrisy. Abhor what is evil. Cling to what is good.*

10 *Be kindly affectionate to one another with brotherly love, in honor giving preference to one another;*

11 *not lagging in diligence, fervent in spirit, serving the Lord;*

12 *rejoicing in hope, patient in tribulation, continuing steadfastly in prayer;*

13 *distributing to the needs of the saints, given to hospitality.*

14 *Bless those who persecute you; bless and do not curse.*

15 *Rejoice with those who rejoice, and weep with those who weep.*

16 *Be of the same mind toward one another. Do not set your mind on high things, but associate with the humble. Do not be wise in your own opinion.*

17 *Repay no one evil for evil. Have regard for good things in the sight of all men.*

18 *If it is possible, as much as depends on you, live peaceably with all men.*

EXPLORING THE MEANING

4) What main ideas do you see in the Romans passage that echo Paul's challenge to the church at Ephesus?

_____

_____

_____

_____

_____

_____

5) How can the existence of different spiritual gifts help bring about unity and growth in the body of Christ? How do differing gifts sometimes spark controversy?

_____

_____

_____

_____

_____

_____

_____

6) What will mature Christian love look like in the body of Christ? Conversely, what would be signs of a church's lack of maturity?

_____

_____

_____

_____

_____

_____

7) Do Paul's exhortations encourage you or discourage you? How does God expect us to carry out all the difficult commands of Christ?

_____

_____

_____

_____

_____

_____

TRUTH FOR TODAY

The church was never intended to be only a building—a place where lonely people walk in, listen, and walk out still alone—but a place of fellowship. In true fellowship Christians don't judge one another; they don't bite and devour each other; they don't provoke, envy, lie to one another, speak evil, or grumble about one another. Since true fellowship builds up, the godly will receive one another, and be kind and tenderhearted toward one another. They will forbear and forgive one another, serve one another, practice hospitality ungrudgingly to one another, admonish, instruct, submit to one another, and comfort one another. That is the true fellowship of Christ's body—life touching life to bring blessing and spiritual growth. The great need of the church has always been spiritual maturity rather than organizational restructuring.

REFLECTING ON THE TEXT

8) The German poet Heinrich Heine once said to some Christians: "You show me your redeemed life and I might be inclined to believe in your Redeemer." How do you respond to this statement? How does it challenge you?

_____

_____

_____

_____

_____

_____

_____

9) Think about your relationships in the body of Christ at your church. What, if anything, keeps you from unity and fellowship? What would it look like for you to "walk worthy of your calling" in these relationships?

_____

_____

_____

_____

_____

10) Do you know what your spiritual gifts are? If not, what steps can you take this week to discover these?

_____

_____

_____

_____

_____

_____

Personal Response

Write out additional reflections, questions you may have, or a prayer.

7

PRINCIPLES OF NEW LIFE
Ephesians 4:17–32

DRAWING NEAR

The New Testament speaks of Christians having a new mind, a new will, a new heart. What does it mean to be a "new creation" in Christ?

_____

_____

_____

If we are new creations, why do we still struggle with sin and hypocrisy?

_____

_____

_____

_____

In what ways have you become "new" since you believed in Christ?

_____

_____

_____

_____

THE CONTEXT

Paul presented to the Ephesians a glorious reminder of their riches in Christ. He treated them to a theological banquet, rich with meaty doctrine. Next, in chapter four, Paul helps them digest this weighty truth. He shows them how to begin living out in practice what is already true of them in principle.

As the Ephesians grasp what God has done for them and in them, they should live transformed lives with a decided difference between their old lifestyles and their new lives in Christ. They should be set apart from those around them. They should stand out. Their interpersonal relationships should be marked by shocking, unearthly attitudes and actions. In a world overrun with bitterness, hatred, deception, and immorality, followers of Christ are to be marked by love, forgiveness, truthfulness, and purity.

Let this remarkable passage challenge you to put the old things behind and begin living out your new identity.

KEYS TO THE TEXT

Put Off the Old/Put On the New: This phrase summarizes sanctification, the continuing spiritual process in which those who have been saved by faith are transformed into Christ's image and likeness. The image Paul uses to describe that process is taking off and putting on clothing, which symbolizes thoughts and behavior. Like one who removes his dirty clothes at day's end, believers must discard the filthy garments of their old, sinful lives, and dress themselves in Christ's righteousness.

UNLEASHING THE TEXT

Read 4:17–32, noting the key words and definitions next to the passage.

Ephesians 4:17–32 (NKJV)

walk (v. 17)—to conduct oneself in daily living

17 *This I say, therefore, and testify in the Lord, that you should no longer walk as the rest of the Gentiles walk, in the futility of their mind,*

18 *having their understanding darkened, being alienated from the life of God, because of the ignorance that is in them, because of the blindness of their heart;*

being past feeling (v. 19)—a reference to the moral dullness or insensitivity that marks unbelievers as they ignore God and their consciences

19 *who, being past feeling, have given themselves over to lewdness, to work all uncleanness with greediness.*

the old man (v. 22)—the worn out, useless, and unconverted sinful nature

20 *But you have not so learned Christ,*

21 *if indeed you have heard Him and have been taught by Him, as the truth is in Jesus:*

be renewed (v. 23)—Used only here in the New Testament, this phrase expresses that at salvation, God redeems a person's mind and gives him or her a completely new spiritual and moral capability.

22 *that you put off, concerning your former conduct, the old man which grows corrupt according to the deceitful lusts,*

23 *and be renewed in the spirit of your mind,*

the new man (v. 24)—a new creation, not a renovation of what was, but an entirely new (in species or character) entity

24 *and that you put on the new man which was created according to God, in true righteousness and holiness.*

25 Therefore, putting away lying, "Let each one of you speak truth with his neighbor," for we are members of one another.

26 "Be angry, and do not sin": do not let the sun go down on your wrath,

27 nor give place to the devil.

28 Let him who stole steal no longer, but rather let him labor, working with his hands what is good, that he may have something to give him who has need.

29 Let no corrupt word proceed out of your mouth, but what is good for necessary edification, that it may impart grace to the hearers.

30 And do not grieve the Holy Spirit of God, by whom you were sealed for the day of redemption.

31 Let all bitterness, wrath, anger, clamor, and evil speaking be put away from you, with all malice.

32 And be kind to one another, tenderhearted, forgiving one another, even as God in Christ forgave you.

corrupt (v. 29)—foul, putrid, rotten, worthless, disgusting

edification (v. 29)—the act of being helpful, constructive, or uplifting

grieve the Holy Spirit (v. 30)—We cause sorrow to the Holy Spirit of *truth* when we act in unholy ways and lie to one another.

1) Paul argues that it is unthinkable for a Christian to act like an unbeliever. What points does he use to make his case?

_____

_____

_____

_____

_____

2) What does Paul mean when he speaks of being "renewed in the spirit of your mind"?

_____

_____

_____

_____

_____

3) Underline each command found in this passage. What are the characteristics of "the new man"?

_____

_____

_____

_____

_____

_____

GOING DEEPER

Consider how the message of Colossians 3:1–17 dovetails with Paul's challenge to the Ephesian church.

1   *If then you were raised with Christ, seek those things which are above, where Christ is, sitting at the right hand of God.*

2   *Set your mind on things above, not on things on the earth.*

3   *For you died, and your life is hidden with Christ in God.*

4   *When Christ who is our life appears, then you also will appear with Him in glory.*

5   *Therefore put to death your members which are on the earth: fornication, uncleanness, passion, evil desire, and covetousness, which is idolatry.*

6   *Because of these things the wrath of God is coming upon the sons of disobedience,*

7   *in which you yourselves once walked when you lived in them.*

8   *But now you yourselves are to put off all these: anger, wrath, malice, blasphemy, filthy language out of your mouth.*

9   *Do not lie to one another, since you have put off the old man with his deeds,*

10 *and have put on the new man who is renewed in knowledge according to the image of Him who created him,*

11 *where there is neither Greek nor Jew, circumcised nor uncircumcised, barbarian, Scythian, slave nor free, but Christ is all and in all.*

12 *Therefore, as the elect of God, holy and beloved, put on tender mercies, kindness, humility, meekness, longsuffering;*

13 *bearing with one another, and forgiving one another, if anyone has a complaint against another; even as Christ forgave you, so you also must do.*

14 *But above all these things put on love, which is the bond of perfection.*

15 *And let the peace of God rule in your hearts, to which also you were called in one body; and be thankful.*

16 *Let the word of Christ dwell in you richly in all wisdom, teaching and admonishing one another in psalms and hymns and spiritual songs, singing with grace in your hearts to the Lord.*

17 *And whatever you do in word or deed, do all in the name of the Lord Jesus, giving thanks to God the Father through Him.*

EXPLORING THE MEANING

4) How do Colossians 3:2 and 10 add to your understanding of being "renewed in the spirit of your mind" in Ephesians 4:23?

_____

_____

_____

_____

_____

5) In practical, everyday terms, how does a Christian "put off" wrong attitudes and habits? How do you "put on" love (Col. 3:14)?

_____

_____

_____

_____

_____

6) What part does knowing God's Word play in transforming us (Col. 3:16)?

_____

_____

_____

_____

_____

TRUTH FOR TODAY

Biblical terminology does not say that a Christian has two different natures. He has but one nature, the new nature of Christ. The old self dies and the new self lives; they do not coexist. It is not a remaining old nature but the remaining garment of sinful flesh that causes Christians to sin. The Christian is a single new person, a totally new creation, not a spiritual schizophrenic. It is the filthy coat of remaining humanness in which the new creation dwells that continues to hinder and contaminate his living. The believer as a total person is transformed but not yet wholly perfect. He has residing sin but no longer reigning sin (Rom. 6:14). He is no longer the old man corrupted but is now the new man created in righteousness and holiness, awaiting full salvation (Rom. 13:11).

REFLECTING ON THE TEXT

7) It has been said that the only reliable evidence of a person's being saved is not a past experience of receiving Christ but a present life that reflects Christ. How well does your life reflect the holiness and goodness of God?

_____

_____

_____

_____

_____

_____

_____

8) What is the Spirit of God saying to you as a result of this study? Do you feel comforted or convicted right now? Why?

_____

_____

_____

_____

_____

_____

9) Write out a prayer, honestly telling God where you are in your faith journey right now. Convey your heart's desire to live in a way that pleases God.

_____

_____

_____

_____

_____

_____

_____

_____

PERSONAL RESPONSE

Write out additional reflections, questions you may have, or a prayer.

_____

_____

_____

_____

_____

_____

_____

_____

_____

_____

_____

_____

_____

ADDITIONAL NOTES

8

WALKING IN LOVE AND LIGHT
Ephesians 5:1–14

DRAWING NEAR

Imagine a man in your church who claims to be a Christian. His testimony sounds legitimate and he has a long history of church involvement. It is common knowledge, however, that this man's life is permeated by a number of glaring, long-term sins. A friend of yours insists that if this man were *truly* a follower of Christ, he would turn away from his sins. Another friend says that we all struggle with various sins and that this man's failings just happen to be among the list of highly visible sins that are frowned upon in Christian circles.

Do you think a person can be a Christian—walk in the light—and continue sinning in grievous ways—walking in darkness? Why?

_____

_____

_____

THE CONTEXT

After describing God's amazing salvation and the incomparable riches that all believers in Christ possess (chs. 1–3), Paul turns his attention to the practical ramifications of the gospel. The old ways are gone; we are "new people." God has gifted us and has called us to live together in a supernatural entity called the church. In unity and love, we are to live to the glory of God. While serving Him on earth, we are to become like Him.

In the passage that follows, Paul describes how conformity to Christ contrasts with conformity to the world. The Ephesian believers lived in a pagan city of spiritual darkness, surrounded by immorality, ungodliness, and decadence. Almost all of them had been saved out of such a background, and they needed to be reminded of what it meant to live in the light.

KEYS TO THE TEXT

Darkness and Light: "Darkness" is the absence of light, and describes the character of the life of the unconverted as void of truth and virtue in intellectual and moral matters. The realm of darkness is presided over by the "power of darkness" (Luke 22:53), who rules those headed for "eternal darkness" (Matt. 8:12). Tragically, sinners love the darkness (John 3:19–21). It is that very darkness from which salvation in Christ delivers sinners. The pure and illuminating light of God's Word exposes all the secrets of sin. God has called his children "out of darkness into His marvelous light" (1 Pet. 2:9).

Imitating God: To "imitate" means to "mimic," or to copy specific characteristics of another person. The example of the heavenly Father and the example shown by Jesus on earth are one and the same, since Jesus came to reveal the Father. Jesus' life was the practical demonstration of His ethical teaching. To His disciples He declared, "I have given you an example, that you should do as I have done to you" (John 13:15). This theme of the imitation of Christ pervades the New Testament letters, especially in the writings of Paul, who instructed his converts to follow "the meekness and gentleness of Christ" (2 Cor. 10:1). Throughout the New Testament, Jesus is presented as the One who left us an example that we should follow in His steps (1 Pet. 2:21).

UNLEASHING THE TEXT

Read 5:1–14, noting the key words and definitions next to the passage.

Ephesians 5:1–14 (NKJV)

fornication (v. 3)—any kind of sexual sin or immorality

foolish talking (v. 4)—A unique word in the New Testament made up of two Greek words: *moros*, from which comes mo-ron = dull or stupid, and *legos* = to speak; intended to describe the conversation of someone intellectually deficient.

coarse jesting (v. 4)—sins of the tongue that include any speech that is obscene, degrading, suggestive, or immoral

has any inheritance (v. 5)—Those with life patterns of habitual immorality, impurity, or greed cannot inherit God's holy kingdom.

1 *Therefore be imitators of God as dear children.*

2 *And walk in love, as Christ also has loved us and given Himself for us, an offering and a sacrifice to God for a sweet-smelling aroma.*

3 *But fornication and all uncleanness or covetousness, let it not even be named among you, as is fitting for saints;*

4 *neither filthiness, nor foolish talking, nor coarse jesting, which are not fitting, but rather giving of thanks.*

5 *For this you know, that no fornicator, unclean person, nor covetous man, who is an idolater, has any inheritance in the kingdom of Christ and God.*

6 *Let no one deceive you with empty words, for because of these things the wrath of God comes upon the sons of disobedience.*

7 *Therefore do not be partakers with them.*

8 *For you were once darkness, but now you are light in the Lord. Walk as children of light*

9 *(for the fruit of the Spirit is in all goodness, righteousness, and truth),*

10 *finding out what is acceptable to the Lord.*

11 *And have no fellowship with the unfruitful works of darkness, but rather expose them.*

12 *For it is shameful even to speak of those things which are done by them in secret.*

13 *But all things that are exposed are made manifest by the light, for whatever makes manifest is light.*

14 *Therefore He says: "Awake, you who sleep, Arise from the dead, And Christ will give you light."*

have no fellowship (v. 11)—literally "do not become a partaker together with others"

expose (v. 11)—The believer's act of confronting and correcting evil in his own life and within the church.

it is shameful even to speak of those things (v. 12)—Some sins are so sordid that even describing them is morally and spiritually dangerous.

1) What does it mean to be an imitator of God? (Underline each reference to godly living.)

_____

_____

_____

_____

2) Paul spells out ways in which the Christian's walk of love contrasts with the counterfeit ideas of love found in the world. What are some of these contrasting actions or themes?

_____

_____

_____

_____

_____

_____

(Verses to consider: 1 John 3:18; 4:7–19)

3) What words of warning does Paul give (vv. 5–7)? Why should we not participate in sinful deeds?

_____

_____

_____

_____

4) What is the significance of the "light and darkness" metaphor used by Paul? What does light do?

_____

_____

_____

_____

_____

GOING DEEPER

Paul expounded often on what it means to walk in the light. Look for further insight as you read Galatians 5:16–26.

16 *I say then: Walk in the Spirit, and you shall not fulfill the lust of the flesh.*

17 *For the flesh lusts against the Spirit, and the Spirit against the flesh; and these are contrary to one another, so that you do not do the things that you wish.*

18 *But if you are led by the Spirit, you are not under the law.*

19 *Now the works of the flesh are evident, which are: adultery, fornication, uncleanness, lewdness,*

20 *idolatry, sorcery, hatred, contentions, jealousies, outbursts of wrath, selfish ambitions, dissensions, heresies,*

21 *envy, murders, drunkenness, revelries, and the like; of which I tell you before-hand, just as I also told [you] in time past, that those who practice such things will not inherit the kingdom of God.*

22 *But the fruit of the Spirit is love, joy, peace, longsuffering, kindness, goodness, faithfulness,*

23 *gentleness, self-control. Against such there is no law.*

24 *And those [who are] Christ's have crucified the flesh with its passions and desires.*

25 *If we live in the Spirit, let us also walk in the Spirit.*

26 *Let us not become conceited, provoking one another, envying one another.*

EXPLORING THE MEANING

5) What new terms for "light/darkness" are used here? How does this passage from Paul's epistle to the Galatians enhance your understanding of 5:1–14?

_____

_____

_____

_____

_____

6) Put in your own words what it means to "walk in the Spirit."

_____

_____

_____

_____

7) What new insights do these passages offer for how you can be *in* the world, but not *of* the world (see John 17:11, 15–16)?

_____

_____

_____

_____

TRUTH FOR TODAY

It is natural for children to be like their parents. They have their parents' nature, and they instinctively imitate their parents' actions and behavior. Through Jesus Christ, God has given us the right to become His children (John 1:12; Gal. 3:26). As Paul declared at the beginning of this letter, God "predestined us to adoption as sons through Jesus Christ to Himself, according to the kind intention of His will" (1:5). Because our heavenly Father is holy, we are to be holy. Because He is kind, we are to be kind. Because He is forgiving, we are to be forgiving. Because God in Christ humbled himself, we are to humble ourselves. Because God is love, as His beloved children we are to walk in love. This ability is not natural, however, but supernatural—requiring a new nature and the continuous power of the Holy Spirit flowing through us by obedience to God's Word.

REFLECTING ON THE TEXT

8) History records that Alexander the Great once discovered a coward in his army, a soldier who happened to also be named "Alexander." The legendary leader confronted the man and thundered, "Renounce your cowardice or renounce your name!" The implication for us is clear. We who bear the name "Christian" need to reflect the character of Jesus Christ. As God's dearly loved child, what are some specific ways you can begin imitating your heavenly Father in your relationships?

_____

_____

_____

_____

9) Do you tend to tolerate evil and look the other way, or do you confront it gently and in love when you see it in your church or world? Why?

_____

_____

_____

_____

10) As you reflect on this passage, what commands do you see that you are not obeying? What sins are you carelessly committing? Ask God to show you where you need to change, and to give you the strength to do so.

_____

_____

_____

_____

_____

_____

PERSONAL RESPONSE

Write out additional reflections, questions you may have, or a prayer.

_____

_____

_____

_____

_____

_____

_____

_____

_____

_____

_____

_____

_____

_____

_____

ADDITIONAL NOTES

9

WISE LIVING
Ephesians 5:15–21

DRAWING NEAR

Imagine finding out that you have one week to live. What regrets or unfinished business would you have? Would you feel you have lived wisely, in a way that honors God? Why or why not?

_____

_____

_____

_____

THE CONTEXT

The apostle Paul wrote to a group of converts immersed in an evil culture. The Ephesian believers were surrounded by pagans who lived for the moment, who rejected the general revelation of God in creation and the special revelation of God in the gospel of Jesus Christ. Their society focused on the worldly and trivial, and indulged their every fleshly whim and desire. This epitomizes foolishness: to ignore the reality of God, to reject His Lordship over one's life, to spurn His gracious offer of forgiveness, to live as though this world were all that is or ever will be.

Lest these old patterns of thinking creep back into the hearts and minds of the Ephesian believers, Paul urgently warns his brothers and sisters in the faith to remember the brevity of this life, the evil, deceptive nature of satanic counterfeits, and the wonderful prospect of walking in and living by the Spirit of God. Only this kind of wise living, befitting our high calling in Christ, can bring joy now and reward in the life to come.

KEYS TO THE TEXT

Holy Spirit: The Holy Spirit is the divine agent who creates, sustains, and preserves spiritual life in those who place their trust in Jesus Christ. Not merely an influence or an impersonal power emanating from God, the Holy Spirit is a person, the third member of the Trinity, equal in every way to God the Father and God the Son. Among the many characteristics of personhood that the Holy

Spirit manifests are: He functions with mind, emotion, and will; He loves the saints, He communicates with them, teaches, guides, comforts, and chastises them; He can be grieved, quenched, lied to, tested, resisted, and blasphemed. The Holy Spirit indwells all believers, illuminating their understanding and application of God's Word. He fills them, seals them, communes with them, fellowships with them, intercedes for them, comforts them, admonishes them, sanctifies them, and enables them to resist sin and to serve God.

Wisdom: In the New Testament, *wisdom* (Greek, *sophia*) is used most often to refer to the ability to understand God's will and apply it obediently. It refers basically to applying truths discovered, to the ability to make skillful and practical application of the truth to life situations.

Unleashing the Text

Read 5:15–21, noting the key words and definitions next to the passage.

circumspectly (v. 15)—carefully, accurately, exactly; carries the idea of looking, examining, and investigating something with great intensity

redeeming (v. 16)—buying back; we are to buy all the time we have and devote it to the Lord

time (v. 16)—not seconds, minutes, and hours, but a fixed, measured, allocated season; that is, our individual lifetimes as believers

do not be drunk with wine (v. 18)—a reference to the drunken orgies commonly associated with pagan worship ceremonies in Ephesus

Ephesians 5:15–21 (NKJV)

15 *See then that you walk circumspectly, not as fools*
      but as wise,
16 *redeeming the time, because the days are evil.*
17 *Therefore do not be unwise, but understand what*
      the will of the Lord is.
18 *And do not be drunk with wine, in which is*
      dissipation; but be filled with the Spirit,
19 *speaking to one another in psalms and hymns and*
      spiritual songs, singing and making melody in your
      heart to the Lord,
20 *giving thanks always for all things to God the Father*
      in the name of our Lord Jesus Christ,
21 *submitting to one another in the fear of God.*

dissipation (v. 18)—excess; that is, a dissolute, debauched, profligate way of living

be filled with the Spirit (v. 18)—to be under the influence of God's Spirit; to be dominated and controlled by the presence of Christ through His Word

psalms (v. 19)—Old Testament psalms put to music

hymns (v. 19)—Songs of praise, different from Old Testament psalms in that these likely praised the Lord Jesus Christ by name.

spiritual songs (v. 19)—probably songs of testimony

giving thanks always (v. 20)—Showing appreciation for who God is and gratitude for what He has done should mark the children of God.

submitting (v. 21)—humbling oneself before others—a characteristic of Spirit-filled believers.

1) Why was Paul so concerned that the Ephesians live wisely?

_____

_____

_____

_____

_____

_____

_____

2) According to Paul, what evidence proves that a person is filled with the Spirit?

_____

_____

_____

_____

_____

_____

_____

(Verses to consider: Acts 2:4; 4:8, 31; 6:3; Rom. 8:9; 1 Cor. 12:13)

3) Paul suggests that wisdom should lead believers to understand and do God's will. How can we know the will of God for our lives?

_____

_____

_____

_____

_____

GOING DEEPER

Consider what King Solomon had to say about living foolishly versus living wisely. Read Proverbs 1:20–33.

20 *Wisdom calls aloud outside; ahe raises her voice in the open squares.*

21 *She cries out in the chief concourses, at the openings of the gates in the city ahe speaks her words:*

22 *"How long, you simple ones, will you love simplicity? For scorners delight in their scorning, and fools hate knowledge.*

23 *Turn at my rebuke; surely I will pour out my spirit on you; I will make my words known to you.*

24 *Because I have called and you refused, I have stretched out my hand and no one regarded,*

25 *Because you disdained all my counsel, and would have none of my rebuke,*

26 *I also will laugh at your calamity; I will mock when your terror comes,*

27 *When your terror comes like a storm, and your destruction comes like a whirlwind, when distress and anguish come upon you.*

28 *"Then they will call on me, but I will not answer; they will seek me diligently, but they will not find me.*

29 *Because they hated knowledge and did not choose the fear of the Lord,*

30 *They would have none of my counsel and despised my every rebuke.*

31 *Therefore they shall eat the fruit of their own way, and be filled to the full with their own fancies.*

32 *For the turning away of the simple will slay them, and the complacency of fools will destroy them;*

33 *But whoever listens to me will dwell safely, and will be secure, without fear of evil."*

EXPLORING THE MEANING

4) In this passage, Solomon personifies wisdom. How does he describe her?

_____

_____

_____

_____

_____

5) Underline each word or phrase that talks about the foolish. How do the foolish react to wisdom?

_____

_____

_____

_____

_____

_____

6) What will happen to those who submit to wisdom and conduct their lives according to her commands?

_____

_____

_____

_____

_____

_____

TRUTH FOR TODAY

To be filled with the Spirit involves confession of sin, surrender of will, intellect, body, time, talent, possessions, and desires. It requires the death of selfishness and the slaying of self-will. When we die to self, the Lord fills us with His Holy Spirit. The filling of the Spirit is not an esoteric, mystical experience bestowed on the spiritual elite through some secret formula or other such means. It is simply taking the Word of Christ (Scripture) and letting it indwell and infuse every part of our being. To be filled with God's Spirit is to be filled with His Word. And as we are filled with God's Word, it controls our thinking and action, and we thereby come more and more under the Spirit's control.

Reflecting on the Text

7) Are you taking the time to read and meditate on God's Word? Why or why not?

_____

_____

_____

_____

_____

_____

8) Carefully review today's passage, noting particularly all the action words and verbs that Paul uses. Would you say that you live a Spirit-filled life? What would living this kind of Spirit-filled life look like for you today?

_____

_____

_____

_____

_____

_____

9) How can you make the most of the time God has given you? In light of the truth that your days are numbered, what trivial activities do you need to drop from your daily schedule? What activities do you need to add?

_____

_____

_____

_____

_____

_____

Personal Response

Write out additional reflections, questions you may have, or a prayer.

Additional Notes

10

GOD-HONORING RELATIONSHIPS
Ephesians 5:22–6:9

DRAWING NEAR

Rank the following descriptions of a person's spiritual maturity from 1–10 (with 1 being the *most* reliable indicator that someone is spiritually mature, 10 being the *least* reliable indicator that someone is spiritually mature).

_____ Has entire New Testament memorized

_____ Has entire New Testament memorized *in Greek*

_____ Has one-hour daily quiet time

_____ Has two-hour daily quiet time

_____ Serves on church missions committee and goes on annual short-term mission trips

_____ Teaches a popular Sunday school class on biblical theology

_____ Graduated from seminary with highest honors

_____ Seldom misses a church function or meeting

_____ Has a strong marriage and lots of healthy relationships

_____ Listens to Christian radio around-the-clock

What is the mark(s) of true spiritual maturity?

_____

_____

_____

_____

THE CONTEXT

Paul's letter to the Ephesians began with three chapters of critical New Testament theology, emphasizing the believer's wealth in Christ. But Christianity is not a collection of abstract doctrines, an ivory tower religion of the mind. Paul contends in chapters 4–6 that true spirituality always reveals itself in the rough and tumble of everyday life.

Jesus simplified God's law to two commands to love—to love God and to love others (Matt. 22:25–29). This is the true measure of our faith. How fully do we love God? Is He uppermost in our affections? Not only that, but how well do we care for our spouses, children, and neighbors? How well do we get along with our coworkers? If our faith doesn't show itself vividly in our interactions with other people, the onlooking world has every right to question the validity of our confession.

Keys to the Text

Submit: To voluntarily surrender one's rights, not out of subservience or servility but out of willingness to function under the other's leadership. Paul introduces his teaching about specific relationships of authority and submission among Christians by declaring unequivocally that *every* Spirit-filled Christian needs to be a humble, submissive Christian (5:21). This is foundational to all the relationships in this section. No believer is inherently superior to any other believer. In their standing before God, they are equal in every way (Gal. 3:28). Proper submission is a key theme of Spirit-filled living. Paul calls all believers to submit to each other; wives are to submit to their husbands, children are to submit to their parents (Eph. 6:1–3). Believers must submit to government laws and ordinances (Rom. 13:1; 1 Pet. 2:13). Younger men should submit to older men (1 Pet. 5:5a). God requires *every* believer to be submissive in the ways He has ordained. In the matter of submission, our primary concern should not be about whom we should be *over* but whom we should be *under*. Humility will prevent the submitting person from becoming burdened, and the person submitted to from becoming overbearing.

Unleashing the Text

Read 5:22–6:9, noting the key words and definitions next to the passage.

Ephesians 5:22–6:9 (NKJV)

22 *Wives, submit to your own husbands, as to the Lord.*

head (v. 23)—This word speaks of God-ordained authority and leadership.

23 *For the husband is head of the wife, as also Christ is head of the church; and He is the Savior of the body.*

24 *Therefore, just as the church is subject to Christ, so let the wives be to their own husbands in everything.*

love your wives just as Christ also loved the church (v. 25)— unreserved, selfless, sacrificial, unconditional love

25 *Husbands, love your wives, just as Christ also loved the church and gave Himself for her,*

26 *that He might sanctify and cleanse her with the washing of water by the word,*

27 *that He might present her to Himself a glorious church, not having spot or wrinkle or any such thing, but that she should be holy and without blemish.*

28 *So husbands ought to love their own wives as their own bodies; he who loves his wife loves himself.*

29 *For no one ever hated his own flesh, but nourishes and cherishes it, just as the Lord does the church.*

30 *For we are members of His body, of His flesh and of His bones.*

31 *"For this reason a man shall leave his father and mother and be joined to his wife, and the two shall become one flesh."*

32 *This is a great mystery, but I speak concerning Christ and the church.*

33 *Nevertheless let each one of you in particular so love his own wife as himself, and let the wife see that she respects her husband.*

6:1 *Children, obey your parents in the Lord, for this is right.*

2 *"Honor your father and mother," which is the first commandment with promise:*

3 *"that it may be well with you and you may live long on the earth."*

4 *And you, fathers, do not provoke your children to wrath, but bring them up in the training and admonition of the Lord.*

5 *Bondservants, be obedient to those who are your masters according to the flesh, with fear and trembling, in sincerity of heart, as to Christ;*

6 *not with eyeservice, as men-pleasers, but as bondservants of Christ, doing the will of God from the heart,*

7 *with goodwill doing service, as to the Lord, and not to men,*

8 *knowing that whatever good anyone does, he will receive the same from the Lord, whether he is a slave or free.*

sanctify . . . cleanse . . . holy . . . with out blemish (vv. 26–27)—The husband has a divine obligation to help lead his wife in purity to conformity with the image of Christ.

nourishes and cherishes (v. 29)—warm and tender affection, attentiveness, and care for needs

be joined to his wife (v. 31)—literally to be glued or cemented together

obey (v. 1)—literally "to hear under"; that is, to listen with attentiveness and with the intent to respond positively to what has been said

honor (vv. 2–3)—to value highly, hold in the highest regard

do not provoke your children to wrath (v. 4)—Do not rule with domineering and authoritarian practices that crush the spirit of a child and cause him or her to lose heart.

fear and trembling (v. 5)—not actual fright but deep respect for authority

eyeservice, as men-pleasers (v. 6)—conscientious labor performed only in the boss's sight, but laziness when his back is turned

giving up threatening (v. 9)— to loosen up, not throw one's weight around in an abusive or inconsiderate manner

9 *And you, masters, do the same things to them, giving up threatening, knowing that your own Master also is in heaven, and there is no partiality with Him.*

1) What statements in 5:22–24 spark controversy? How does a careful reading of this entire section (vv. 22–31) refute most, if not all, of what the modern feminist movement claims about Christianity's view of women?

_____

_____

_____

_____

2) Why is the marriage bond sacred (5:29–32)?

_____

_____

_____

_____

3) What is the God-given role of a Christian wife?

_____

_____

_____

_____

_____

4) What is the God-given role of a Christian husband?

_____

_____

_____

_____

Going Deeper

In a related passage, Paul teaches more about honoring God in our relationships. Read Colossians 3:18–4:1.

18 *Wives, submit to your own husbands, as is fitting in the Lord.*

19 *Husbands, love your wives and do not be bitter toward them.*

20 *Children, obey your parents in all things, for this is well pleasing to the Lord.*

21 *Fathers, do not provoke your children, lest they become discouraged.*

22 *Bondservants, obey in all things your masters according to the flesh, not with eyeservice, as men-pleasers, but in sincerity of heart, fearing God.*

23 *And whatever you do, do it heartily, as to the Lord and not to men,*

24 *knowing that from the Lord you will receive the reward of the inheritance; for you serve the Lord Christ.*

25 *But he who does wrong will be repaid for what he has done, and there is no partiality.*

4:1 *Masters, give your bondservants what is just and fair, knowing that you also have a Master in heaven.*

Exploring the Meaning

5) What do you think it means to submit?

_____

_____

_____

_____

_____

6) List some of the primary ways parents tend to "provoke" and "discourage" their children.

_____

_____

_____

_____

_____

_____

7) In the first century, Paul saw many abuses in slave/master relationships. What principles from the twin passages in Ephesians and Colossians can you draw for modern-day working relationships?

_____

_____

_____

_____

_____

_____

_____

Truth for Today

There are no classifications of Christians. Every believer in Jesus Christ has exactly the same salvation, the same standing before God, the same divine nature and resources, and the same divine promises and inheritance (Acts 10:34; Rom. 2:11; James 1:1–9). But in matters of role and function God has made distinctions. Although there are no differences in intrinsic worth or basic spiritual privileges and rights among His people, the Lord has given rulers in government certain authority over the people they rule, to church leaders He has given authority over the church, to husbands He has delegated authority over their wives, to parents He has given authority over their children, and to employers He has given authority over employees.

Reflecting on the Text

8) Growing within our culture is a widespread rebellion against and distrust of authority. How do you usually respond to someone in authority over you?

_____

_____

_____

_____

_____

9) How can authority be a wise and good thing? How can authority be harmful when abused?

_____

_____

_____

_____

_____

_____

10) Given what you've studied about God's intention for husbands, wives, children, and parents, what encourages you? What convicts you?

_____

_____

_____

_____

_____

_____

11) Specifically and practically, what can you do to be a better employee/ employer this week?

_____

_____

_____

_____

_____

_____

Personal Response

Write out additional reflections, questions you may have, or a prayer.

_____

_____

_____

_____

_____

_____

_____

_____

_____

_____

_____

_____

_____

_____

_____

_____

_____

_____

_____

_____

_____

_____

11

Spiritual Warfare

Ephesians 6:10–17

Drawing Near

The faithful Christian life is a battle—warfare on a grand scale—because when God begins to bless, Satan begins to attack. Have you, or someone you know, experienced what you would call "spiritual warfare"? If so, how did you—or they—respond? Explain what happened.

_____

_____

_____

_____

The Context

Paul's description of the true Christian, described in chapters 1–3, and the faithful Christian life, 4:1–6:9, lead him to an exposition on spiritual warfare in 6:10–20. If we are walking worthy of our calling, in humility rather than pride, in unity rather than divisiveness, in the new self rather than the old, in love rather than lust, in light rather than darkness, in wisdom rather than foolishness, in the fullness of the Spirit rather than the drunkenness of wine, and in mutual submission rather than self-serving independence, then we can be absolutely certain that we will have opposition and conflict.

The good news is that God does not leave His children unprepared or unprotected in this cosmic conflict. This passage is a heartening reminder of all that God has done and all that we must do to win the victory. In Christ, not only can we withstand the devil's assaults, but we can also defeat the diabolical forces that are arrayed against God and His church. The gates of hell cannot stand against us!

Keys to the Text

Spiritual Warfare: The true believer who lives the Spirit-controlled life can be sure to be in a spiritual war. The fight is a supernatural one against Satan, whose schemes are propagated through the evil world system over which he rules, and are carried out by his demon hosts. The Lord provides His saints with sufficient armor to combat and thwart the adversary. Paul uses the common armor worn by Roman soldiers as the analogy for the believer's spiritual defense and affirms its necessity if one is to hold his position while under attack. Ultimately, Satan's power over Christians is already broken and the great war is won through Christ's crucifixion and resurrection, which forever conquered the power of sin and death (Rom. 5:18–21). However, in life on earth, battles of temptation go on regularly. The Lord's power, the strength of His Spirit, and the force of biblical truth are required for victory.

Unleashing the Text

Read 6:10–17, noting the key words and definitions next to the passage.

Ephesians 6:10–17 (NKJV)

be strong in the Lord and in the power of His might (v. 10)—Believers must rely completely on God's omnipotence to win the battle.

stand (v. 11)—to stand firm, in a military sense; to maintain a critical position while under attack

wiles (v. 11)—schemes; the Greek word from which comes the English term "methods." Carries the idea of craftiness, cunning, deception.

wrestle (v. 12)—hand-to-hand combat

principalities . . . powers . . . rulers . . . spiritual hosts of wickedness (v. 12)—A description of the different strata and rankings of invisible, supernatural demons and evil spirits who are part of the devil's empire.

shod your feet (v. 15)—Roman soldiers wore boots with nails (cleats) in them to help brace their feet in all terrains. For the Christian, the gospel of peace with God gives sure footing and a sound foundation.

shield of faith (v. 16)—The word is the Greek term for the large 2.5 x 4.5 foot shields carried by soldiers to protect their entire bodies. As long as Christians place their trust in God, they will be protected.

fiery darts of the wicked one (v. 16)—In ancient times, arrows were often tipped with cloth, covered with pitch and ignited; the idea is that our faith affords us protection against the many temptations of the devil.

10 Finally, my brethren, be strong in the Lord and in the power of His might.

11 Put on the whole armor of God, that you may be able to stand against the wiles of the devil.

12 For we do not wrestle against flesh and blood, but against principalities, against powers, against the rulers of the darkness of this age, against spiritual hosts of wickedness in the heavenly places.

13 Therefore take up the whole armor of God, that you may be able to withstand in the evil day, and having done all, to stand.

14 Stand therefore, having girded your waist with truth, having put on the breastplate of righteousness,

15 and having shod your feet with the preparation of the gospel of peace;

16 above all, taking the shield of faith with which you will be able to quench all the fiery darts of the wicked one.

17 *And take the helmet of salvation, and the sword of the Spirit, which is the word of God;*

the helmet of salvation (v. 17)—protects the head, for Satan attacks a believer's assurance of salvation with his weapons of doubt and discouragement

the sword of the Spirit (v. 17)—The truth of Scripture, the only weapon that a Christian should carry into battle.

1) What does Paul mean when he states categorically that our fight is "not against flesh and blood"?

_____

_____

_____

_____

_____

_____

_____

Underline each word and phrase that describes our enemy and his/its activity.

2) What protective (defensive) pieces of armor are children of God given in their ongoing struggle with the forces of evil? What offensive weapons are we given with which to wage war?

_____

_____

_____

_____

_____

_____

_____

3) Why does Paul emphasize the concept of *standing* (vv. 11, 13–14)?

_____

_____

_____

_____

_____

GOING DEEPER

Consider the example of Christ in the famous account of His temptation in Luke 4:1–13. Note carefully how He waged spiritual warfare.

1 *Then Jesus, being filled with the Holy Spirit, returned from the Jordan and was led by the Spirit into the wilderness,*

2 *being tempted for forty days by the devil. And in those days He ate nothing, and afterward, when they had ended, He was hungry.*

3 *And the devil said to Him, "If You are the Son of God, command this stone to become bread."*

4 *But Jesus answered him, saying, "It is written, 'Man shall not live by bread alone, but by every word of God.' "*

5 *Then the devil, taking Him up on a high mountain, showed Him all the kingdoms of the world in a moment of time.*

6 *And the devil said to Him, "All this authority I will give You, and their glory; for this has been delivered to me, and I give it to whomever I wish.*

7 *Therefore, if You will worship before me, all will be Yours."*

8 *And Jesus answered and said to him, "Get behind Me, Satan! For it is written, 'You shall worship the Lord your God, and Him only you shall serve.' "*

9 *Then he brought Him to Jerusalem, set Him on the pinnacle of the temple, and said to Him, "If You are the Son of God, throw Yourself down from here.*

10 *For it is written: 'He shall give His angels charge over you, To keep you,'*

11 *and, 'In their hands they shall bear you up, Lest you dash your foot against a stone.' "*

12 *And Jesus answered and said to him, "It has been said, 'You shall not tempt the Lord your God.' "*

13 *Now when the devil had ended every temptation, he departed from Him until an opportune time.*

Exploring the Meaning

4) What method did Jesus use to defend Himself against the attack of Satan?

_____

_____

_____

_____

_____

_____

_____

(Verses to consider: Matt. 4:1–11; Luke 22:44)

5) Read 2 Corinthians 10:3–5. What extra insights into spiritual battle do you find in this passage? What is the tone of this passage? Why?

_____

_____

_____

_____

_____

_____

6) Read 1 Thessalonians 5:6–8. What should be the Christian's frame of mind?

_____

_____

_____

_____

_____

_____

_____

Truth for Today

It is easy for believers—especially in the Western world, where the church is generally prosperous and respected—to be complacent and become oblivious to the seriousness of the battle around them. They rejoice in "victories" that involve no battles and in a kind of peace that is merely the absence of conflict. Theirs is the victory and peace of the draft dodger or defector who refuses to fight. They are not interested in armor because they are not engaged in war. God gives no deferments or exemptions. His people are at war and will continue to be at war until He returns and takes charge of earth. But even the most willing and eager soldier of Christ is helpless without God's provision. A Christian who no longer has to struggle against the world, the flesh and the devil is a Christian who has fallen into sin or into complacency. A Christian who has no conflict is a Christian who has retreated from the front lines of service.

Reflecting on the Text

7) What does this study teach or remind you about spiritual warfare? How aware are you of the cosmic conflict going on between God and His enemies?

_____

_____

_____

_____

_____

8) In what specific ways/areas does Satan most often tempt (wage war against) you? Why those ways?

_____

_____

_____

_____

_____

9) How successfully do you resist him? What new ways do you need to put on your armor and stand? Ask God to give you the grace to stand in His strength and to fight as you should.

_____

_____

_____

_____

_____

_____

_____

_____

PERSONAL RESPONSE

Write out additional reflections, questions you may have, or a prayer.

_____

_____

_____

_____

_____

_____

_____

_____

_____

_____

_____

_____

_____

_____

_____

Additional Notes

12

A Praying Church
Ephesians 6:18–24

Drawing Near

In six brief chapters Paul has presented a balanced view of what it means to know and serve God—including setting guidelines for what the church, the body of Christ, should be. If you could develop "the perfect church" according to Paul's description of the body of Christ, what items from the following list would you include? (Put a check mark beside your choices.)

_____ a state-of-the-art, multi-million dollar facility (debt-free)

_____ a gifted, talented, unified staff

_____ a congregation enthusiastic about and trained for evangelism and missions

_____ a prayer ministry composed of faithful saints interceding at all times

_____ a national TV/radio ministry featuring solid biblical exposition

_____ a top-notch education program for children and youth

_____ a premier pastor who has best-seller books

_____ a vibrant inner-city outreach

Which "features" did you pick, or not pick, and why?

_____

_____

_____

_____

The Context

Paul's letter to the Ephesians is concise in its language yet comprehensive in its scope; profound in its theology yet practical in its application. Ephesians begins by lifting us up to the heavens and ends by pulling us down to our knees. Paul focuses our attention fully on God and on our continued need for His help. God's armor is neither mechanical nor magical. We cannot simply take hold of it on our own and expect it to automatically perform supernatural feats. Our divine gifts—marvelous as they are—are impotent without the divine Giver. We need to offer corporate, continual, and fervent prayer. This is the note Paul ends on.

KEYS TO THE TEXT

Prayer: The Greek word translated "prayer" (also in 1 Thess. 5:17) is the most common New Testament word for prayer and refers to general requests. The word translated "supplication" refers to specific prayers. Paul's use of both words suggests our necessary involvement in every form of prayer that is appropriate for the need of the moment. Another type of prayer is intercessory prayer, meaning "to intercede on behalf of another"; the word referred to bringing a petition to a king on behalf of someone else. Prayer is fitting at any time, in any posture, in any place, under any circumstance, and in any attire. It is to be a total way of life—an open and continual communion with God. After having embraced all the infinite resources that are yours in Christ, don't ever think you're no longer dependent on the moment-by-moment power of God.

UNLEASHING THE TEXT

Read 6:18–24, noting the key words and definitions next to the passage.

Ephesians 6:18–24 (NKJV)

supplication (v. 18)—specific petitions

in the Spirit (v. 18)—in the name of Christ, consistent with His nature and will

being watchful (v. 18)—staying awake, being vigilant

that utterance may be given me (v. 19)—Paul's request is not for prayers for his personal well-being or physical comfort but for boldness to continue proclaiming the gospel, regardless of the cost.

ambassador (v. 20)—an envoy who represents a government

in chains (v. 20)—Paul wrote this letter while under Roman imprisonment.

18 *Praying always with all prayer and supplication in the Spirit, being watchful to this end with all perseverance and supplication for all the saints—*

19 *and for me, that utterance may be given to me, that I may open my mouth boldly to make known the mystery of the gospel,*

20 *for which I am an ambassador in chains; that in it I may speak boldly, as I ought to speak.*

21 *But that you also may know my affairs and how I am doing, Tychicus, a beloved brother and faithful minister in the Lord, will make all things known to you;*

22 *whom I have sent to you for this very purpose, that you may know our affairs, and that he may comfort your hearts.*

Tychicus (v. 21)—See Acts 20:4–6; 2 Timothy 4:12; Titus 3:12.

comfort your hearts (v. 22)—literally "to call alongside" so as to bring encouragement

23 *Peace to the brethren, and love with faith, from God*
  the Father and the Lord Jesus Christ.
24 *Grace be with all those who love our Lord Jesus*
  Christ in sincerity. Amen.

1) In this short passage, what does Paul teach about the:

variety of prayer?

_____

_____

_____

_____

frequency of prayer?

_____

_____

_____

_____

power and manner of prayer?

_____

_____

_____

_____

2) Why does Paul choose *not* to use this occasion to solicit prayer for his own release from prison? What does that tell you about him?

_____

_____

_____

_____

(Verse to consider: 2 Tim. 2:9)

3) How would you answer someone who argued that "praying in the Spirit" (v. 18) means praying in an ecstatic language or "tongue"?

_____

_____

_____

_____

GOING DEEPER

Luke 22:39–46 records the prayer vigil kept by our Savior in Gethsemane during His darkest hour. Consider how Jesus braced Himself for the onslaught of Satan.

39 *Coming out, He went to the Mount of Olives, as He was accustomed, and His disciples also followed Him.*

40 *When He came to the place, He said to them, "Pray that you may not enter into temptation."*

41 *And He was withdrawn from them about a stone's throw, and He knelt down and prayed,*

42 *saying, "Father, if it is Your will, take this cup away from Me; nevertheless not My will, but Yours, be done."*

43 *Then an angel appeared to Him from heaven, strengthening Him.*

44 *And being in agony, He prayed more earnestly. Then His sweat became like great drops of blood falling down to the ground.*

45 *When He rose up from prayer, and had come to His disciples, He found them sleeping from sorrow.*

46 *Then He said to them, "Why do you sleep? Rise and pray, lest you enter into temptation."*

EXPLORING THE MEANING

4) How does this passage contribute to your understanding of prayer as a weapon in our war against Satan?

_____

_____

_____

_____

5) Clearly, prayer is one of the critical components of Christianity, yet many believers seem to regard prayer as an occasional luxury. Why?

_____

_____

_____

_____

_____

_____

6) Read 1 Timothy 2:1–4. What insights do you learn for why Christians need to pray widely and continually?

_____

_____

_____

_____

_____

TRUTH FOR TODAY

In his *Pilgrim's Progress*, John Bunyan tells of Christian's weapon called prayer, which, when everything else failed, would enable him to defeat the fiends in the valley of the shadow. Prayer is the closing theme of Ephesians, and though closely related to God's armor, it is not mentioned as part of it because it is much more than that. Prayer is not merely another godly weapon, as important as those weapons are. All the while that we are fighting using the girdle of truth, the breastplate of righteousness, the shoes of the gospel of peace, the shield of faith, the helmet of salvation, and the sword of the Spirit, we are to be in prayer. Prayer is the very spiritual air that the soldier of Christ breathes. It is the all-pervasive strategy in which warfare is fought. Jesus urged His disciples to pray always and not to lose heart (Luke 18:1). He knows that when the battle gets hard, soldiers easily become tired, weak, and discouraged. In the struggle with Satan, it is either pray or faint.

REFLECTING ON THE TEXT

7) Through the centuries, Christian leaders have realized how crucial prayer is:

"When God intends to bless His people, the first thing He does is to set them a-praying." *Matthew Henry*

"When we work, we work, but when we pray, God works." *Unknown*

"A church without an intelligent, well-organized, and systematic prayer program is simply operating a religious treadmill." *Paul Billheimer*

"The less I pray, the harder it gets; the more I pray, the better it goes." *Martin Luther*

"Satan laughs at our toiling, mocks at our wisdom, but trembles when we pray." *Unknown*

What do these quotes, and more importantly, the Scriptural texts studied in this lesson, teach or remind you of as you contemplate your own habits of prayer?

_____

_____

_____

_____

_____

8) Compare the content of Paul's prayers to the content of most prayers that you hear today. What differences do you notice?

_____

_____

_____

_____

_____

9) What have you learned from Paul's prayers that has helped you know better how to pray for other people?

_____

_____

_____

_____

_____

10) As this study of Ephesians ends, list several new things you have learned about yourself and about God.

_____

_____

_____

_____

_____

PERSONAL RESPONSE

Write out additional reflections, questions you may have, or a prayer.

_____

_____

_____

_____

_____

_____

_____

_____

ADDITIONAL NOTES

Additional Notes

ADDITIONAL NOTES

ADDITIONAL NOTES

Additional Notes

Additional Notes

Additional Notes

ADDITIONAL NOTES

ADDITIONAL NOTES

ADDITIONAL NOTES

ADDITIONAL NOTES

ADDITIONAL NOTES

Additional Notes

ADDITIONAL NOTES

Look for these exciting titles by John MacArthur

Experiencing the Passion of Christ

Experiencing the Passion of Christ Student Edition

Twelve Extraordinary Women Workbook

Twelve Ordinary Men Workbook

Welcome to the Family:
What to Expect Now That You're a Christian

What the Bible Says About Parenting:
Biblical Principles for Raising Godly Children

Hard to Believe Workbook:
The High Cost and Infinite Value of Following Jesus

The John MacArthur Study Library for PDA

The MacArthur Bible Commentary

The MacArthur Study Bible, NKJV

The MacArthur Topical Bible, NKJV

The MacArthur Bible Commentary

The MacArthur Bible Handbook

The MacArthur Bible Studies series

Available at your local Christian Bookstore
or visit www.thomasnelson.com

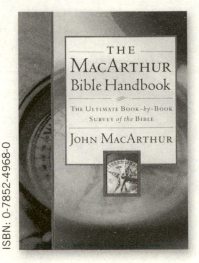
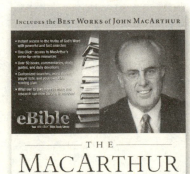